APOCALYPTIC ACAPPELAS

Akor Emmanuel Oche

APOCALYPTIC ACAPPELAS

(poems)

Akor Emmanuel Oche

Copyright ©2018 *Akor Emmanuel Oche*

ISBN: 978-978-964-187-1

All rights reserved.
No part of this book may be reproduced, distributed, stored in a retrieval system or transmitted, in any form or by any means, electronic, electrostatic, magnetic tape, mechanical, photocopying, recording or otherwise without prior written permission from the Publisher.
For information about permission to reproduce selections from this book, write to info@wrr.ng
National Library of Nigeria Cataloguing-in-Publication Data.

Printed and Published in Nigeria by:
Words Rhymes & Rhythm Limited
Suite C309, Global Plaza Plot 366, Obafemi Awolowo Way, Jabi District, Abuja, Nigeria.
08169027757, 08060109295
www.wrr.ng

Contents

DEDICATION	7
Acappella	9
—Il buon tiempo vera—	10
Ocean of Songs	12
Choice	13
Malnourished	14
In the age of the Demons Rule	16
Do not ask	17
In bleeding Rhythms of the Sole	19
Count your Scars, Name them One-by-One	20
Robbed OF Childhood	21
What Mama Said	22
Scars, Cicatrix, Sorrow	23
A Silent Journey from Innocence	24
How to Cuddle a Girl like Me	26
Lozenge	28
Black Background	29
Flower girl	31
JailBird	32
Jasmine	33
LoTus	34
Amidst Libation Chants, we call thee Home with Pleas	35
Sailor Sail Home	36

The Convert 37
A Song for Ihuoma 38
DÁDÁ 39
Expression 40
Perhaps 41
Song, Toil 42
Away 43
Blue Air 44
Oro Ko Lopin Si O 45
Apocalypse 46

DEDICATION

I dedicate this to bla bla bla and bla bla bla because of bla bla bla and bla bla.

I am
the last testament
of an apocalypse
coming like a thief
in the *black-outs* of time
to steal the souls of gods
in exchange for words

Acappella

silence sings a silent song silently
through this monody from the diaphragm
of mockingbirds encoding every
splendor in their synchronized
tune; a wail here, a brawl there,
then a chirp.
birds whistle—at night, birds sing.
so does mother.
she tunes a wail
for each new burden carried,
she never opted for this.
father lied.
true lovers don't die young.

—Il buon tiempo vera—

I die twice over each time mother looks into my
eyes
In gazes bearing ignited end ropes of warming
canons
exploding into questions from her crisped lips
folded
Into layers of a rhythmic dance to the sound of age.

about my age, twenty-seven broken years in
memory,
on a night uncertain as this, a man, naked all
round,
danced around the hours of her prime body in
sequenced
beats bombing into white dropping songs. I was
born

conceived as the last testament of pleasure between
souls
birthed in baptisms of fire, water, silence & love
two months & sixty-two days to his sudden death
on a voyage to the north of greener pastures &

all he left was a will of hunger, a hectare of hopeful
songs
& a basket full of mothers prayers pouring as the
fall
into the bergamot clouds of heaven's eavesdropping
ears

atonement today, tomorrow redemption, next a
plea for our daily bread.

here in my father's house, a man stares at me from
the eyes
of a black & white photography, his face resembles
mine
in every grace & in the depth of my heart I hear his
voice,
unannounced like December winds, say to me carry
on
—*Il buon tiempo verra*— the good times will come.

Ocean of Songs

on this sail
of rowing dreams
we are learning to spell
mothers like P A D D L E S

eyes like scarecrows
bereft of splendor
broken into fragments of nostalgia
of memories plainer than reality.

on each morning of decaying dreams
we are learning her enunciations
from slipping tongues that ask
*'when is the coming of the
promised better days'*

Choice

outside solitude soliloquizes
In garbs of lament songs.
sun shines above heads
pivoted on necks bent down.

time spins on wheels of pains;
eyes are wondering where to look next.
pent-up petrifactions skid down
In gradients of unanswered prayers.

tangents of strut dreams
grovel along curves of unimaginable situations.
grimace stupefies the bourgeoisie,
adjunct volition is denied the acolyte.

In the aborigine of black out evenings
metamorphosed into societal decadence,
the pen heads—as I— like moonless nights –
squalor in solitude.

Waiting
Wishing
Wailing

Malnourished

mild noon-time breeze purls,
as sunrise rays clang the bell
for ideal men to get to work.
each shrugging the dust of
last night's hustle off the shoulders.

a poet embraces time, taking
calculated steps along a mile
In search of answers. there
thoughts of her rush in again
in photograph like flashes.

Inikpi, your image is embroidered
on my mind, every junction, every
bend I walk reminds
me of your scrawling flesh;
a cellophane on dried bones.
how did the world get so unwise,
how did the earth get so tasty
for your blood child?

death is a wish not granted,
you pray her come, but she never takes heed.
happy are the ones who fall into eternal rest
you say: "go. prepare ye the way of the just.
for if today I do not fall
of this shanty, of this crowd,
if today, immorality does not find me an errand
girl,

if this war doesn't break loose
on my mortal body
then tomorrow, I shall greet the echelons
with stones, if my words bear no meaning."

In the age of the Demons Rule

a poet searches for consolation
with cheeks resting on palms
frosted from absent tears.

inept, his being jolts
to endless jamborees of fear & weeping
for the many burdens tasseled on his neck,

he searches for providence
at the cleavages of poetic verses,
he seeks the face of god earnestly in

blank white sheets full of unseen hope,
full of riddles steeped in ascending rows,
full of prayers & lament songs.

heaven is womb-less, heaven is barren,
her uterus cannot birth further prophesies
for these days of austerity.

sailing on we row with the waves of time,
life is a road leading to unequal places,
death or breath, fate is fate.

Do not ask

a broken boy
how he learnt to engrave
his name on empty walls.
full of questions,

haven't you heard it said of
shattered mirrors, that they carry
a thousand reflections?

see!

a boy cries in the distance,
his voice fades into echoes
too faint for this noisy world to hear.

&

ask not a shrivel girl
how she learnt to condone
chauvinistic blooms in
heat seasons.
haven't you heard it said of time,
that it changes everything
including people?

see!

a girl cries in the distance
for space to be who she is,

her body is water, her soul, a sea
fitting for all who dare to swim.

In bleeding Rhythms of the Sole

to be a poet is to be lost
In the thousand shattered things
falling off the flapping wings of a
monochromatic bird whose
apparition is in a black hue.
she rests upon her adumbration whistling —
It is to worship your body, Mama,
offering particular burnt sacrifices,
each to a forbidden region on your landscape:
palms turgid with supplications,
lips, the bearer of bags full of enchantments,
feet approaching your altar
In bleeding rhythms of the sole
masticating this barren earth to fertility;
an unblemished totem for worship.
to be a poet mama, is to cram
the names of all your contours;
Imperfect curves entwined together
In resonance. It is to be a devotee
to the religion that you are.

Count your Scars, Name them One-by-One

for some, home is where dying is living one more day
in a house full of hungry looking faces & babies whose
voices grow dim with the breaking of new dawns.

it is so for me too. & every time my feet navigate
through purrs of this city heading home, I
lost happy nerves to wrinkles, frowns, brows & wishes—

brother taught me to love my sores wherever,
on this broken body, they may be. & my scars?
he reminded me to number them, each according to its

day of manufacture; that sores & scars are
what makes a man what he is—a man—his voices echo
through the vast winds each time I look into little sister's eyes.

mother is a fresh testament of flesh turning
iron made ductile by the hammering palms of time
hers is a story for new days: a gospel worth many pages.

Robbed OF Childhood

too many nights & sunrise in darkness,
& I have become a metaphor for dumb men
eating in silence, words falling from gluttonous lips.
too many nights... & I hack back to lost days
when at twelve, I became a man for the family.
father's exit left for us all a pool to fill with
waters fetched from years of struggles.
seven years after a robbed childhood,
seven stolid years down this forlorn road—
I am still here sulking in silence.
it hasn't gotten any better yet; it never does.

What Mama Said

sangfroid glances pierce the earth//In flooding torrents.
foots scamper for their covens//It is dusk, a time for darkness.
the soil is for the sons//at night time, at times of survival.
I have learnt the rudiments since//I was ten; get a gun, wear a mask,
frighten someone and get the cash//but today another dawn slowly beckons,
to meet my feet on the run//sirens blaring, touch lights beaming...
I recall mama's words//she said *'son, never let this poverty turn you into a criminal'*
Lord have mercy//I never planned for this.

Scars, Cicatrix, Sorrow

of these stories written on your
eyelids, I may never get to read
their finished lines; how you
master the touch of burning
fingers tracing marks on your
cheeks, how you learn
to forgive those palms
that batter you.
I may never get to play the
chords of your vulnerability;
how you pluck each key and
a note of wails is heard, how
each diameter of your breast
understands this routine
mastered from constant
practice; grab the baby, cover
him with your body & let
him rain down his blows on
you. I may never get to recite
the full lyrics of struggles
before sex each night, how you
fight your man to let go, then
break into surrender until
what is left is the dirge of
crackling bed sounds, how you
still live with Hades when
Heaven is close by, just few
kilometers out the door.

A Silent Journey from Innocence

shortly after puberty at sweet 16,
you had discovered the secrets of pleasure
on the handbook of the hedonist,
you had learnt what the lines on your palms are
meant to grip
a twitch at one nipple,
a suck on the other, the short silence, then loud
moans...
you had mastered the rudiments
exactly as uncle Tony said you would...
you remember him, his lanky structure.
but most importantly, you remember
the reassuring seductive tone of his voice
& how he used to whisper into your honey ears
sweet nothingness coated with instructions
as his tongue savored the juice between your
thighs,
then there was Taye; at 18, your sexpert of a
boyfriend,
he taught you how to recite psalms according to
moans;
a verse for a verse, than fire
then hot squirting, then laughter, then silence.
it always ended in silence.
first time at 15, it was guilt and hate, a
reminiscence
first time at 17, it was freedom and the rebirth of
lost innocence in the clinched arms of a false lover.

now at 20, you have discovered a new path
to the stream of endless songs trapped
beneath your protuberant hips.
your palms abandon the nipples
and journey down your glory hole
strumming it into milkiness & songs.

How to Cuddle a Girl like Me

first begin with her hair;
fondle each strand gently & feel
the empty holes on her scalp where
beautiful hair strands once laid, now plucked out
by her father while dragging her on the kitchen floor.

then proceed to her lips;
kiss them gently
so you don't ignite, again,
the abusive words they
once said to Dan, her stepbrother,
for wanting to eat a fruit from a garden he never pruned .
now, hold her breast firmly,
suck of the milk
that belongs to her aborted child.
she was fifteen then, he would have been eight by now.

caress her skin in a purr,
do not rush. take it slow,
so you can feel all the marks;
all the hurdles that are
testaments of her broken being.

then visit her honeycomb;
watery, molten, & fresh.
do not fret at your first feel of its depth,

that too is a testimony of the character
of many frustrated men, who at some point
cajoled it to climax.

Lozenge

   sharp cuts by heavens granite each
   bend blended to the most accurate
   proportion of the diviner's fingers,
    your lips, curly in perfect synch
    with clouds dancing to songs
   red as the sky on an angel's death.
  when last did they taste the scarlet
  encasing of fresh fleshes naked at the
  parting crossroad of words. Lozenge
  glistering to shrapnel of candle lights
  as echoing tenors dis-virgin the night.
  I sometimes remember lost memories,
    fragments buried on strange
   smiles, people, moments, songs
  smeared on drizzles of time falling
upon eternity; the debris rescind into packages
  meditation for contemplated nostalgia;
 the voices, I reminisce too, soft, cajoling,
 ret in mixture of two blends, one dark,
 the other sublimating along an ounce of
  phonologies across the Niger area.

Black Background

night is the song of a mocking bird that ridicules its
reflection.
perhaps you may think her a puzzle lost in too
many colors,
or a room full of windows that opens only to
sunshine within.

this is how she narrates her story, birthing life into
the silent cadavers of whistles.
perhaps she should wipe off the tear drops with the
back of her palms today—you say
*'the heart is a road of concrete steel, nothing breaks
a broken thing twice'*

perhaps she cried that very minute within twinkles
when he soaped her thighs plodding her oven into
protrusion.
,,,

you fall into her story,
& wonder how a pedophile thinks,
you curse, you lament, you pause
in reflection & exactly at that moment you
remember

the voice of your neighbor's daughter pleading with
you in between soft moans
"uncle stop, I am…" you were only 20 then, she, 16

it felt so good at the time. you could swear an
oracle's head that she wanted it,
you could kill to prove that she enjoyed it,

'her moans sang of pleasure than pain' so you said
in your heart over the years but
today, half way through this interview, abandoned
memory haunts you.

Flower girl

every time a palm explores
the contoured curves on your
body—every time a touch be-
comes an awaking psalm of buried
memories, you feel it again, you
feel him again. Every time you
inhale the smell of an hibiscus
you feel it again, you remember
what it smelled like on that day
when a sharp pain tore through
your tights and left you tremble-
ing in pain mixed with pleasures
all wrapped up in rivers of blood.

JailBird

(for chibuzo)

they said you dreamed of freedom,
seeking answers to why caged birds sing,
wanting to know if tomorrow you will be free.

they said you were a song,
the wind, your music—
that you hummed of drifting years,
that you hummed of chains.

that your eyes were that of a boy
lost in the heat of the hustle,
lost in curtains of hope
looped in torrents all about.

that you emptied that poison's
bottle without bothering
to drop us an exit song, maybe
on paper, maybe on your skin with blood.

freedom was all you longed for,
freedom is all you have now!
sing JailBird!
Sing brother. Sing!

Jasmine

just an hour before 3 O'clock—
entrapped for numberless seasons—
a new song escapes your throat
into courtyards of blooming air.

Love & Jasmine,
green in flowery temperatures that scourge
daylight into sour litanies of endless fear—
in your voice is the songs of heaven sung

smoothly in serenading silence,
of winds & suns and predictions.
on your shoulder, earth burdens
her expressions of unperturbed sorrows.

here, an hour away from 3 O'clock;
5 sodden steps from apocalyptic acappellas
you burst forth into tatters & tongues —
every word uttered

drowns one more cubit of your sanity in
waters of prophesies—whose waves fill our ears
as a crowd gathers abroad in sympathy.

Jasmine, flower, love. every December
in the pale presence of harmattan chills, I die
again,
killed by the songs your lips sing.

LoTus

two things;
a hairpin of memory
whose metal core carries forgotten
debris of you,
a bead
of two distinct
colorings with six strands
attached to the epicenter of one half of your
earrings—
fuming of you.

I wish they leave me now
in the ambience of silence.

I only covert four things always
drifting away one after another:

a river of flourishing LoTus,
the four other wings of everything,
many things, a single thing
too much a number to numerate:

1— the stillness in your stare.
2—an ocean of your smiles.
3— my fingers brushing the wind off your face
4—your lips begging me to come back.

Amidst Libation Chants, we call thee Home with Pleas

Okolobia!
the night has gone with the
bags of darkness that accompanied her—

yesterday was a puzzle,
whose secrets have been discovered by today.
will you return home now?

Okolobia! It is you whose name we splutter
on harmattan soured lips
when we pour libation to Oweicho.
please come back home from
the land where your ancestors lost their dignity
to the whips of the slave masters.

Okolobia! come home to the soil into whose
stomach your umbilical cord was buried.
the fire that burnt your father's hut
has been tamed by the healing balms of time,
come home & rebuild its ruins.

Sailor Sail Home

we see the footprints of our childhood
stampeded on this loess soil,
on this land whose trajectories we know,
on this savannah planes arable for matching boots,
this mountain barricades surmounted by pointing
riffles.
& along with this servile body is a dirge.
sing it to the merriment of passers-by.
Native!
we once sang the songs of neo-nomadic men
when the price of a sheep was banquet for the host
community.
Native!
nostalgia serves you a flagon as you roll and row.
'sir! Here, take a sip'
of mud houses roofed with elephant grass,
of swords sounding the drumbeats of war,
of women bathing in the streams unclad,
of men whose valor touches the sky.
we see our footprints on this mystical floor.
Native!
we sail, you sail, but never reach the corridors
of politicking negritude in sprees.
sailor, sail home
to the place where waters are dark rooms
& the sea a castle.
we see the footprints of our childhood
stampeded on this loess soil,
on this land whose trajectory we know.

The Convert

I dig deep into the coffers of my ancestry,
paying homage to Alekwu's priest.
standing to gaze for hours
at the bank of Ogbano river.

the deeper I look,
the lesser I see.
the much I learn,
the little I understand.

our fathers are wise,
they left us with parables
to chew in life & in death,
to leave for our children to chew.

hacking back to my roots,
I become a pilgrim in search of truth.
I become a convert
to the ancient path,
the path that is true.

A Song for Ihuoma

(on reading Elechi's 'The Concubine')

Ihuoma's waist is a metaphor,
vivacious virtue,
swinging succulently
against the raging wind storming into submission
many immaculate eyes watching her perform—
a rare & pure beauty to behold.

Ihuoma is a thousand years of history
told in tears from the coven
of a bleeding writer's pen—
calling men to rethink their roots.

Ihuoma is the cry of a woman chained
with the metal-manacles of culture
with a beauty fast fading away,
not in the arms of a childhood lover,
but beside the grave of five dead husbands.

DÁDÁ

forte et forte,
ash to ash. cremated,
dust to dust sent
by ill winds blowing without direction.
we commit you to mother earth,
a blossoming flower stampeded
by the feet of your kindred spirit.
you came again,
(but stayed a bit longer than usual,
maybe for the love you found
in this den of comic memories)
to laugh at our existence;
enigmas of vanity.
to laugh at how we touch this body,
your body; a celestial media
communing with erstwhile beings,
gone from our shores to worlds of the reaper
and now after beating her frail being;
emblem of childbirth, cicatrix
of sons who never cross the twentieth mark—
to the age long danced, you have gone,
gone to return once again
as the child with cursed tassels for hairs.

Expression

Is the songs of this dissident resonating in the
market place,
echoed from a voice so cracked that it disappears
into the distance.
lost to the force of winnowing winds.

It is the songs the sea sings to its banks
when falling tides hum an intimate melody.
It is the gentle whistling of the mocking birds at
twilight
serenading the atmosphere of sleeping lovers.

expressions are bitter mothers cursing the nights
that procreated burdens for sons.
they are bitter mothers cursing the 21st century
kind of kings
who care less about the subjects they govern.

expression is this album of threnody
chanted from the center of the village square,
resounding & reverberating until they cleanse this
nation
of the curse embedded on her scalp.

Perhaps

on the long run
Beer bottles are the answers
to many unanswered prayers,
for men still drown in the watery
layers of their own creation.

here am I in a city
where no one sins in sincerity
& denial is the muse of the acolytes.
& we ask, what is more wrong than
doing wrong the wrong way.

perhaps virgin ecstasies
are still altered in brothels
under the ritual rite of lingering
& many offer supplications at
the requiem of their climaxing cleavages

here am I in a country
where all we ask for are
eloquent speeches & long
explanations for the evil done to us

or maybe, just maybe
our silent sentiments & murmuring grunts
will grant them further warrants to loot us.

Song, Toil

my bed is an ocean
& my pillow; the sea
paddling down emotions
from rivers in my eyes
into her flowing banks
in wishes, fantasies, tears & songs—

my feet; a stranger
on th' same soil that birthed its so(u/l)e...
yet I stagger on.
on, on daily repentance from
lost sins forgotten underneath the struggling rides
of time.
for survival, sailing unchartered waters,
finding new beginnings, picking up embers
of burnt Wonderings, creating heaven from hell
where & when we do not see one.

Away

like bird songs wrenching air
with painful pleasures from
waves breaking free into erect pinnacles
hungry for masturbatory redemption – we sail.
every drop of time
precipitates gloomy seconds
from face-pours familiar with sorrow...
life is too entwined to obey patterns,
often she becomes an offspring of blue songs
whiffing from ravenous speakers, earphones,
toilet thoughts, dancing kids,
mad chatters between beer bottles, & guitar.
every new walk on dreadful paths put fear on her heels
as depression takes the face of a lover
purling away like ideal birds on a half broken
mahogany branch.

Blue Air

I have learnt how to die
from the flickers of
burning coal;
Crimson at birth,
bathed by air
& then back to black charcoal.

I peel off my skin at dawn
shedding its colors out
on blue air,
counting a thousand
years in one stare at the stars,

as one who have & still
falls and falls and fa...
until it is out of its own body.

Oro Ko Lopin Si O

tomorrow is buried in the intimacy of today's
twilight dance, tippy and euphoric, sending
calculated jolts down our forbidden spines.
our loins know no restriction nor reserved
areas where the sonorousness of night drums
are barred from reaching. Drums whose
membranes
are cuddled by the ample fingers of the Alagba;
spirit in the claddings of a mortal's skin. yesterday
came with good tidings immersed in a pool of
silence & stars that broke the secret of ancient
Drums. today is another litany of songs
from the market place chanted by feet
destined to last the moment—here now,
gone later like you whose voice during farewells
is the most accurate cannon. the most accurate
killing machine. but Ewa, Zahara, *oro ko lopin
Si o!* my dialogue with you has no end.

Apocalypse

this I no!
of this truth I am set in—
the road to pared-ice
is two wrong to be write.

night is a song of circles
twilling into the fabrics of
dawn in half-contoured rhythms
of a revolving moon-song

&
I
am

the last testament
of an apocalypse
coming like a thief
in the black-outs of time to
steal the souls of gods
in exchange for words.

AKOR EMMANUEL OCHE is a Nigerian poet, critic and essayist. He is the Secretary of the Africa Haiku Network and C.E.O of OCHEBOOKS: writing, entrepreneurship and publishing consultancy firm which also specializes in art collection and dealing.

Akor Emmanuel Oche